Moira Andrew

Man In The Moon

a collection of poems

Indigo Dreams Publishing

First Edition: Man In The Moon
First published in Great Britain in 2014 by:
Indigo Dreams Publishing
24, Forest Houses
Halwill
Beaworthy
Devon
EX21 5UU

www.indigodreams.co.uk

Moira Andrew has asserted her right under the Copyright, Designs and Patents Act 1988 to be identified as the author of this work.
©2014 Moira Andrew

ISBN 978-1-909357-37-2

British Library Cataloguing in Publication Data. A CIP record for this book can be obtained from the British Library.

Designed and typeset in Palatino Linotype by Indigo Dreams.
Cover design by Ronnie Goodyer of Indigo Dreams.

Printed and bound in Great Britain by Imprint Academic, Exeter.

Papers used by Indigo Dreams are recyclable products made from wood grown in sustainable forests following the guidance of the Forest Stewardship Council.

For Fiona and Jen,
for NL
and in memory of Allen.

CONTENTS

Man In The Moon

a collection of poems

In a dark room

Lying in the dark it's easy
   to remember things
you thought you'd forgotten,
the smoky red nap of train
   seats in carriages
labelled 'Non-smoking'.

Like ghosts, long-hushed
   sounds whisper –
morning ash being riddled
from the grate, wailing sirens,
   my mother's heartbeat
steps on the attic stairs.

Smells too, seep through cracks
   and under doors,
my dentist dad's minty hands,
Gran's cinnamon toast, but
   try as I might
I can't get faces into focus.

My eyes squeeze shadows
   from corners, pummel
them like potter's clay, hoping
to mould them into likenesses –
   without success. Nor
can I reinvent long-silent words.

In my room's quiet darkness
   past and present
are on the same side and
the dead dance foxtrots,
   flirt and kiss, never once
looking back to fill in the dots.

Red roses

Fairies don't like red, unlucky,
they say, dangerous, blood
and fire, a going-down
of the sun.

To us it's the colour of love, red
roses, hearts on Valentine's Day –
you revelled
in all that.

Your own was wonky, reducing you
to a breathless wreck some nights,,
your puffer
a bedfellow.

It took a Naming Ceremony
to persuade you into a red shirt –
Just this once,
you said.

Fairies had the last laugh, blood
leaked from your cracked heart,
shed its red petals
in a rush of love.

The key

The man forged a key
opened a door
in the sky, well,
you take it
that's where he went
not that you know
for certain – after all
you've seen neither hilt nor hair
of him from that day
to this.

You woke up
one morning
kissed the man, stretched, said
I'd better make a move
cleaned your teeth, showered
put down a bowl
of cat-food, made toast,
coffee, not knowing
he'd already turned his key
in the lock.

Dead man's shoes

Knock-kneed, they wait
in the dust of the bottom shelf,
abandoned, almost forgotten.

They've waited at lights, urged
the old red Vauxhall into action,
accelerated, braked.

They've waited under beds
listening to the song of springs,
the murmuring of lovers.

They've waited for seven years,
unworn, unpolished, heart-
breaking as photographs,

the imprint of feet a memory
of the man, of miles walked,
of Cornish paths explored.

They wait, like patient dogs, for
the sound of his voice, disappointment
in each sagging lace.

Black on black

in ragged black coats,
they bookend one another
high on bare branches

two couples wintering
together, morning
to evening

from time to time
they shuffle closer
wings almost touching

at night
they roost in my head
feathering my eyelids

downloading a darkness
to come
black on black

and I save
their macabre dance
to a web page

for future reference

Man in the moon

You cuddled me close last night –
arms swaddling me in sleep, radio
keeping us in touch with wars
and hurricanes and everyday disasters.

I so wanted to tell you
about my treacherous eyes,
but night got in the way
and you were more interested
in my breasts, the smell of my hair.

Maybe you were listening, maybe not –
the trouble is, I've lost my touch,
in fact I'm not entirely sure you lived,
I know you died – I was there.

My bare feet trawl the depths
of our bed, lust after you, chill –
(the cat doesn't do love-ins)
dreams fade, you're out of focus
words won't work anymore –

there's no arguing with a man from the moon.

Thief

A raven
swoops down
and steals my sight
while I dream
of poppies
and sunflowers
gazing
wide-eyed
from French fields

You stand
in your blue
short-sleeved shirt
trying
to wave it away.
My eyes
you say
have let me down!
Mine too.

Not to worry

Don't worry, the consultant says,
peering at me through thick glasses,
You're not going blind!

I hadn't thought of that, just
the nuisance of a blurred grey daisy
pattern in my left eye.

A man telephones. He remembers
me as I used to be, slim, single, sexy.
It's a bugger, this growing old, he says.

Got a jazz gig on Thursday,
I hear the smile in his voice – *for
the Church roof, any excuse for a blow!*

He loathes his carer's role, making
suppers, brewing tea, *I'm not cut out
for this kind of thing … I wish …* silence …

Hope you get good news … good news?
about the eye. Yes, I say, hope so …
Anyway, try not to worry … stroke the cat,

pretend it's me. The buzzer trills,
I replace the receiver, turn down
the heat under my soup pan,

a ripple of joy at his call, a thread
of dread when I think of my eye.
Like the man said, *It's a bugger!*

Fingers

How many can you see?
a gloved hand
three wiggling fingers
not cruel
just curious
at the age of six or so

Aunt Jess loved to walk
going at a trot
all the way
to Cathkin Braes
on Grandad's left-hand side
her arm resting
on his elbow

dark glasses gave her away
apart from that
no-one would have guessed

she had a few tricks
up her sleeve
putting two fingers
into the milk jug
so it didn't overflow

I find myself
doing just that
as I top up
a flower vase

when I can't read the chart
with my left eye
the nurse waggles her fingers
How many can you see?
she asks.

Frightening the fairies

They bustle around,
poke thorns into my eyes.
I hear them laughing,
black cloaks fluttering

like wings in the wind.
I'm told it takes seven things
to make them go away.
I consult my list.

First I need *fire*, a match?
(I don't smoke) a candle flame?
Sorted – the gas heater,
turned to its highest setting.

Red I can do, my teacher's pen,
Chambers' dictionary, a t-shirt.
I had fantastic red shoes once,
but they're long gone.

Salt, no problem, I'm a cook.
Steel, a carving knife, sharp enough
to scare the living daylights
out of any evil-doer.

Dirt's easy, a trowelful of soil.
And *black?* I wear it, the
creatures tease me with it, black
being their colour of choice.

I count my fairy-frighteners
each a talisman against
the coming dark – just number 7's
magic to track down.

But it doesn't feature –
my torn-off list ends at six.
Back to the drawing board,
to night in my eyes.

Red geraniums

Aunt Kate
and red geraniums
go together

I remember
rubbing the leaves
so my fingertips
smelt green

window boxes
heavy with flowers
balanced on the sill
at a precarious angle

pots on the step
scattered red petals
and a door
that didn't fit

I remember
Aunt Kate's long white apron
I have no memory
of Uncle Andrew

just the sound
of the sea
and an empty wheelbarrow

Sister

I remember being ushered into our spare room,
the solemnity of it all, coal fire huffing in the grate,
sun flooding through sash windows, my mother
propped on pillows – in the middle of the afternoon –
why not in her own bed at the top of the house?

A grey-haired nurse in armour-plated uniform
appeared to be in charge. I'd never met her –
what business did she have bossing Dad and me
around? She produced this real live baby from
a crib in the corner, *Your little sister,* she said.

I could look at her, but must not touch. *Now,
a kiss for Mum and off downstairs with you!
Mummy needs her sleep* – in the daytime?
Dad took my hand and did as he was told.
We found Gran supervising things the kitchen.

My whole world was in a spin, but like children
do, I adapted. The baby became a permanent
fixture. She had a name, Eleanor. We grew up
under the same roof. All I know of her now,
is a scrawled signature on a Christmas card.

Brush work

The sun empties out its light,
splashing walls and easels,
the bare floor. We stare at
fallen flower pots and feathers
in jars. We narrow our eyes,
chew pencil ends and sigh.
Neat, we are, in navy skirts,
blue tops and ties,
> *Jean and Kathleen,*
> *Maeve and me.*

Small sounds nudge the silence,
shoes scuff, adolescent stomachs
murmur and we grumble a bit.
We dip hog-hair into water,
mix puddles of paint in clean
white saucers, make first
tentative marks. We measure,
thumbs on brushes,
> *Jean and Kathleen,*
> *Maeve and me.*

We are different, we Higher Art
girls. Others slog over maths
and Latin verse, chemistry and
French. In our sky-high eyrie Miss
Meldrum brings us shortbread,
Miss Liston talks of love. And,
in secret society, we dream our
tomorrows, not knowing,
> *Jean and Kathleen,*
> *Maeve and me.*

We have grown old, we Higher Art
girls – and I read in the paper
they've pulled the building down,
our bright rooftop refuge
ripped across and across like
some abandoned painting. Yet,
we pose together in time, we four,
framed in sunlight,
>   *Jean and Kathleen,*
>   *Maeve and me.*

The hat box

in her heyday
my mother wore hats
didn't feel dressed
if she went out
bare-headed
not even running
across the road
to Winnings' Stores
and later on
to Safeways
with its brightly-lit aisles
wide wire trolleys
hours of gossip

holidays in Cornwall
were a different matter
there she sported
a daring navy-blue split-skirt
Aertex shirts
her hair Marcel-waved
the modish felt hats
(brown black ink-blue)
tucked away at home
in round white hat-boxes
taking up space
on the top shelf
of the wardrobe

I don't remember
my mother smiling much
she took life
pretty seriously –
worrying her *raison d'etre*
about dad me my sister
if she was wearing
the proper clothes –

I do have one photograph
she and four friends
(complete with cloche hats)
crammed into an old Austin 8
and she's laughing

Grandpa's treasure chest

he examines each one
with intimate care
rolling it round
in his big earthy hands
picking prying poking
like a monkey
searching her baby for fleas
selecting only perfect specimens
polishing each smiling face
with a clean cloth
wrapping it in a twist
of greaseproof paper
and placing it
in an old dressing table drawer

I try to help, *This one Grandpa*
I say scooping up
a hard greeny-brown apple
its skin rough lustreless
Can you no see, child?
he says pointing out a tiny wormhole
Go and badger your Gran
she hovering in the kitchen doorway
waiting for him to explode
in exasperation – his Russets
are an annual labour of love
needing total concentration

huffing and puffing
his white moustache
wet with spittle
Grandpa ranks the last apple-parcels
tight as Terracotta Warriors
Gran and I barely breathe
as he performs a last rite
covering the drawer

with gently tucked-in newspapers
before bearing the whole thing
up to the attic
in ceremonial procession
Gran steadying the steps
me drinking in the nutty bittersweet smell

Echoes

My grandmother had a passion
for earrings. She kept them
in a box with five squeaky drawers
that stood on the dressing table
        throughout my childhood.

I stood on tip-toe, my pickpocket
reflection tripled, ran fingers
through beads of coral, jade, lapis
lazuli, held their glittering fall, like
        icicles, against my face.

My mother, straight-laced
Church of Scotland, had no time
for such fripperies. Hats, yes. Earrings,
no. I can still hear the tut-tut
        of her abrasive tongue.

But me, I couldn't wait for
the day I'd be grown-up enough
to swing extravagant jewelled globes
from my ears, catching the light
        as I moved my head.

He knew my obsession, bought me
moonstone and silver, every flash
in the mirror as I brush my teeth,
spray my hair, an echo of grandmother
        and the lavender smell of her skin.

Crossroads

Of course, I was young
and image-conscious –
well, that's my excuse.

I'd met my grandmother
by chance out shopping
down Stonelaw Road.

She shifted her brown
leather bag from one hand
to the other, readied herself

for a good gossip. The
bag bulged, stalks of pink
rhubarb sticking out the top.

Just out for a few messages,
something for Grandpa's dinner –
you know what he's like!

I did. You didn't mess
with Grandpa's meals – he
demanded them frequently

and on time. *And what*
about you on this fine day?
Glimpsing my new boyfriend

on the opposite pavement,
I hopped with impatience.
Mustn't keep you, dear …

And she raised her cheek
for a kiss. I couldn't be seen
to be kissing my Gran –

not in the street in broad
daylight – so I just patted
her hand, fled across the road,

my teenage integrity intact.
Wrong choice. My grandmother
died that night, unkissed.

Iris

In my head I try to resist – my hand
ignores the warning signs, dips
into the pot – £2.50 and a wrap of spears
is mine.
          They won't last, a voice
in my mother's Scottish accent.
Like I've done all my life, I ignore it,
drive home, flowers on the passenger seat,
a blade of colour showing.
                     In a slim vase,
they stand tall and green, slowly unfurling
into blueness, peacock-eye petals lighting
up the room.
            Flowers are my addiction
(they were my grandmother's drug of choice).

They put iris on her grave – for years
I couldn't look their glory in the face.

Loch Lomond

My friend squeezes back tears.
I can't bear to think about it –
Mum gone, Aunt Chris on her own.
The loch appears and disappears,
its waters stealthy with secrets.

I concentrate on parking close
to the cottage wall. We step out
into near-stillness, a shush of waves,
the call of an oyster-catcher.
Aunt Chris erupts down the path.

My dears! She smothers Elsa
in a bear-hug, gathers me into the
huddle. *You'll be needing a drink,*
tea? coffee? something stronger?
A tough cookie is Elsa's Aunt Chris.

Of course, she misses her sister.
What's done is done, she says.
We toast our toes by the kitchen range,
the kettle hums, a wall-clock ticks,
waves lap stones by the garden gate.

Aunt Chris, serene in her aloneness,
waves us off. I glance at my friend,
Better? I ask. She nods, *How about you?*
I take a moment, *If Mum died, I'd cope,*
not if it was Dad … not if it was Dad.

Fruitcake

we stand together
on the back step
out of sight
licking spice from our fingers

Even better than your mother's
Dad says
But don't let on –
she'll never forgive me

not a cake at all
sultanas, brown sugar, currants
baked in crisp pastry
(Mum's speciality)

I've pinched her recipe
added cinnamon, apples
a hefty sprinking of ginger
Just up my street, Dad says

Mum tuts
You were sent to try me!
her skills lie in the kitchen
mine in words, in paint

and here I am
beating her at her own game
I can't blame her
for having a go at me

co-conspirators
Dad and me
brushing away
telltale crumbs

Some things never change

When night takes hold
my father taps me
on the shoulder. His fingernails
are short, disinfectant-clean – I'd
recognise them anywhere, just from
the smell.
        He looks at the new old me,
puzzled – no, shocked – at what he sees,
after all, he's fully twenty years my junior
and it's no joke coming across this
bus-pass daughter whose dead husband
he's never met.
        But he's unchanged,
neat RAF-type moustache, stone-blue eyes
still deep and clear.
        Drink? I offer,
Thought you'd never ask. I pour two fingers
of Bells, top it up with water. He mooches around
riffling through books, fingering things,
clocks my emails spinning on to the screen.
I google 265 Stonelaw Road, zoom
in to the garden, mostly decking where
Mum once had a washing line.
        *Thought I'd seen
it all when those fellows landed on the moon,*
he says. He opens the back door, shivers
in a chill wind, downs the last of his drink.
He gazes up at the night sky, every star
reassuringly in place.
        He checks his watch,
the very same watch that lives in the top drawer,
minus a battery, stilled these many years. *Must
make a move – your mother will be wondering
what's keeping me. You know what she's like.*

I do, still the boss – some things never change.

Riddle

Hold me, like a talisman,
snug in the bowl of your hand.

Look at me, the russet moon
dropped from a star-barrow.

Listen to me, to my new-borns
rattling (if you're the lucky one.)

Smell me, the perfect pomander,
studded with a single juniper-gem.

Taste me, fruit of the gods,
crisp-cold as a March morning.

Flowers for the table

I cut hydrangeas
their fierce blue a welder's torch
forging memories.

Fire flowers

we spoke only once
unlikely paper turds
that we were
you shook the packet
we promised you flames
you listened
scattered us by the wall
left us to get on with it
we warmed our cockles
drank deep

came June
a hint of green
nothing much at first
you turned your back
found us
hooking our feet
climbing
climbing
a spiral bud here
a pointed tail there

two
then three
five six seven
till you ran out of fingers
and we exploded
in a firework
of peppery green
a starburst of orange
yellow deepest gold
blazing five-petalled
exuberance

up and over the wall
        hot enough
                to burn your eyes
but deep in our open mouths
        a scarlet streak
                a pearl of rain
                        a flicker of lust

Tuning in

a gurgle of waves
an idle of blues
a bustle of bees

wearing
the late afternoon
like faded jeans

tuning in
to the scrunch
of sandals on sand

and the intricate design
of Dove's-foot Cranesbill
close up

Norway from the tourist bus

you run out of colour words
        green doesn't do it
nor does jade
        sage   reseda   malachite

        green invades your eyes
on every side   above and below
        green vertiginous slopes
slung round the mountain's shoulders
        a green tree-lined valley
like an unknotted scarf trailing its fringes
        in the secret depths
            of the fjord
        green mosses
edging white suicidal waterfalls
grass-thatched huts beading the shore

your retina   like your vocabulary
can't cope with this glut of greenness

snow whitewashing mountain peaks,
the white ship on black waters – from
        oil-paint to pen-and-ink

Winter trees

flex
their writing muscles
lean elbows on the hill
stare at the sky
in no hurry of course
creative juices stir
in their own good time

they
sharpen nibs on
outstretched branches
rummage in a selection
of inks ... black is best
as night falls ... grey-green
for early morning

then
wince as birds step
on their knuckles ... at last
heads-down in the wind
they work on their scripts
recovering bedrock truths
as they do every spring

Feather

I found it on the path
soft as sleep
its shaft bone-strong

like love
with its pale underside
its toughness

maybe I'm thinking
of marriage
from cool morning kiss

to raised voices
when each tests
the other's wing-span

for that moment
teetering on the edge
of flight

ruffled plumage
is soothed under
the duck-down duvet

a whisper *didn't mean it*
a tickle of toes
a tentative kiss *me neither*

and the singing begins

First love

I fell in love
when I was eight
or thereabouts
a wedding
a man
all booted-and-suited
paying attention
to the child
in a blue dress.

I remember
wineglasses
filled with sparkle
grown-up conversation
knowing laughter
filtering the air
above my head.

You're the girl for me
the man said
laying a hand
flat on my back –
unsettled by his touch
by his milk-pale eyes
I was hooked.

Home time
a storm of confetti
he wrapping
his wife's shoulders
in a flimsy lilac shawl
never once
looking back
at the child
in the blue dress.

Compliment

Met Fred the other day,
one old colleague to another
Art department, remember?

I do, although it's going on
for thirty years since we worked
together. The poetry plaque

Fred made hangs on the wall
in my hall – a leaving present
from the College.

We talked about the old days,
about you, he goes on. *Fred says*
you had the best legs in Craigie!

It makes me feel good, lets me
ignore my wonky eyes,
brings back a forgotten flutter.

All-night party

Late nights have never been my thing,
so I've no idea how I coped, dozed
on the boyfriend's shoulder I expect
to brighten up in the small hours.

We listened to records, to the boyfriend's
party-piece, *Honeysuckle rose,* played
with speed and flair. We jived, smooched,
snogged, changed partners, drank wine.

One of the boys grilled bacon for baps.
I remember the sizzle, the smell, that first
salty bite. I remember a girl sitting at the top
of the stairs, the sound of her crying.

Behind drawn curtains, the group fractured
into pairs, less laughter, more fumbling.
I remember the door opening to birdsong,
to the liquid light of a summer morning.

Black dress

I had this black dress once,
an off-the-shoulder affair
that made me look sexy – or
so I thought, glimpsing myself
in the mirror. True, men
looked at me differently,
calculation in their eyes – even
my husband – and I felt
I had the world at my feet.
In real life I was mother, wife,
teacher and thoroughly unsexy,
but quite another woman in
that little black dress. I could
dance till two in the morning,
waltz, jive, quickstep with
the best of them. I discovered
I could fall in love again, make
a man's eyes light up – not
my husband's, as it happened –
the little black dress no longer
important as it slid to the floor.

Something special

There's something special
about love in the afternoon
when the sun spills out
its yellow juice and
small domestic sounds
go on underneath our
window, the tuk of
fallen clothes-pegs,
washed dishes settling
in the rack, next door's kids
squabbling like gulls.

There's the frenzy of
tearing off clothes, shirt,
trousers, top, skirt, the
fumbling for tissues,
the muffled laughter,
lying naked, exhausted,
on top of the duvet.
There's the shutting-out
of the cat, kisses stolen
in the soft glow of afternoon,
the decadence of it all.

There's the jump of
complicity when the bell
rings, the what-would-the-
neighbours-say syndrome,
the relief when it's only
the window cleaner come
to collect his money.
Another world, one
coloured in honey-yellow
light, the afternoon
languid now, untrammelled.

Aftermath

after it's over
we lie coiled
all-in-one
a dark talking-time
words tripping over
one another
in indulgent richness
and we laugh
at silly jokes
only we would understand
and my hair tickles your nose
so you sneeze
slip out of me
and our jigsaw pieces
unlock
into separate arms
and legs and toes
and we watch
an orange streetlight
felt-tip the edge
of our curtained window
and listen to the rain
till the cat reckons
it's safe to jump
back on the bed
to burrow
into the narrow gap
of warmth
          between us

Tea ceremony

I hear the doorbell, voices,
a few unfamiliar mumbled words.
                                             I slip
deeper into the hot suds, fragrant with expensive
toko-juzu, sip my drink. A knock, my husband
puts his head round the door, *A summons,* he says,
our new neighbours.
                              73, you mean?
                                    The very same.
                              Now, this minute?
                                    Wouldn't take no for an answer.
                        You didn't tell them I'm in the bath?
                                    My Japanese doesn't stretch that far.

I drain my gin-&-tonic, wrap myself in a towel,
go downstairs, stand by the window, watch
the deepening snow, relieved to be home from
a morning tutoring in the Brecon Beacons.
My husband checks his watch, *Better get a move on.*

                                             We dodge
across the road, bow, remove our shoes, follow
the couple into the living-room, bare of furniture,
except for a square table, barely ankle-height. We squat
on silk cushions, smile, make small-talk and the man translates.
Thigh muscles screaming, I get up, admire a set of dolls
displayed on red shelves.
                              Hina-Matsuri? I ask.
The woman beams with delight. *You know Hina-Matsuri?*
(I've used it in a book of festivals, so I'm on to a winner.)

                                    Time for tea, the man says.
The couple disappear into the kitchen. My husband gets up
to stretch his legs, rubs his cold hands, *Saki?* he guesses.

A steaming silver kettle
and delicate tea-cups, black, bone-thin, are placed on the table.
We sit back down, wait. The woman brings in a giant-size jar
of *Nescafe* and four jam doughnuts. The man hands them round
with pride, *From Tesco,* he says.

Kitchen drawer

Not for kitchen cutlery the luxury
of plush-lined pockets, regimented
wedding-present canteens – they come
as a hotch-potch of oddments, mixed race,
uncertain backgrounds, remainders, survivors.

They're placed in wire trays
in some kind of order, teaspoons with
teaspoons, vegetable knives together, blades
facing away, but what about rarely-used
things, like the pizza-cutter, kept *just in case?*

I tip them out, spoons and knives, forks,
whisks, tin-opener, bottle-opener, skewers.
I clean the drawer with a kitchen wet-wipe, dry it
with a paper towel, wash the mismatched cutlery.
They all have their stories, these left-overs –

grandmother's spurtle, a wooden stick, unused,
          (I don't like porridge),
her child-sized rolling pin, a favourite utensil,
          (makes my daughter smile),
a silver teaspoon marked DNB,
          (my mother's newly-wed initials),
a new potato peeler,
          (the old one has lost its bite),
a champagne cork,
          (from our 10th anniversary)

knives and spoons from other people's kitchens –
two tiny coffee-bean spoons,
          (the others lost to my ex-husband),
the only tablespoon,
          (bequeathed by my mother)
a large silver fork of unknown ancestry,
five refugee dessert-spoons
          (from my husband's ex-wife's widower?)

Job done, I replace the clean cutlery,
spoon by spoon, fork by fork,
a new-fangled plastic net
for unscrewing reluctant tops
cheek by jowl with bone-handled left-overs –
scissors, bread-knife and wooden spoons
easily accessible at the front –
and push the drawer closed.

The musician

It's taking such a long time, she says,
The trouble is, every step is down.
A silence at the end of the line.

> I never knew him as a well man,
> the musician whose fingers flew over the keys,
> I never saw him with two working arms.

He's home now, of course. A pause,
I keep the radio on all the time, Classic FM,
not that he notices much these days.

> I mumble in reply – what can you say?
> *He's doubly incontinent, you know – but we've*
> *got carers, so I don't have to deal with that.*

I remember how he enjoyed red wine
– a rare treat, when we came to dinner –
how he tucked, one-handed, into his food.

> *I get out two afternoons a week … I go*
> *to Ruth's, walk round M&S … not to the men's*
> *department, I couldn't bear that.*

I know how she feels. Neither could I.
But my man's death was quick, here
one minute, gone the next. *Visitors?* I ask.

> *Not so's you'd notice … I just wish …*
> she stops … *I'm grieving, he's breathing.*
> We say good-bye, hang up.

Remembrance

At this 11th hour on this 11th day of November,
Big Ben is followed by silence, but Radio 4
doesn't do silence as a rule. I sit down, tea-towel
in hand, close my eyes.

        I try to think proper
Remembrance Day thoughts, soldiers dying in
Afghanistan – what a waste – poppies appearing
all over the telly, (except for Jon Snow, of course)
but they elude me.

        I listen to wind in the trees,
imagine last leaves giving up the ghost, skirling
to the ground. I hear cars on the A39, the whine
of an ambulance, wonder briefly about its payload –
hope it's not serious.

        I'm not good at
this thinking to order – maybe I need practice –
the Quakers have it down to a fine art, they say,
but I don't know any Quakers, (Sheila Hancock
doesn't count.)

        I've got it! – *hooded* – the word
I need to finish a winter poem. I think about
Allen, dead these seven years, panic – I can't
picture his face – maybe he wasn't real?

        It's a long
two minutes. I think about the cat, she's dead too,
my father, my first husband – not that any of them
is poppy-worthy. My foot itches. A gull, in big boots,
prances across the conservatory roof.

        The newscaster
cuts in, the Euro, the economy, Helmand. I'm released
to grab the label on an old silver bag, (filled with shells
for a children's workshop), *For my darling Moira,* it reads,
All my love at Christmas, Allen xx – it's OK, he did exist.

        I get on with drying the dishes.

Starry starry night

They're talking about you again,
Vincent. You're on their radar.
You know that painting you did,
the one with black cypress trees
corkscrewed against a night sky?

Not that they were black to you,
of course, nor was the violent sky.
Black, you said, *is a mixture*
of blue and violet, yellow and
green. How right you were.

In your terrible passion, you painted
non-stop, creating an ocean of sky
clouds like storm-tossed waves.
But, as you say, the sky's not
truly black, not by a long chalk.

More a vaudeville of colour.
And those stars. Your frisbee stars
haven't half stirred up the scientists.
They're measuring them, Vincent,
lining them up with the planets.

Not for them awe at the citron-yellow
you used to make your tumbling suns.
They're more into celestial sleuthing.
pinpointing the very place you stood
to paint that starry starry night.

You've got them into a right royal
lather. Me too. It's your vigour,
your outrageous colour that gets to me.
It still hits the spot, Vincent. In a
clockwork universe, colour matters.

Fishing

I landed you
in my net,
but in those days
I was lucky

ignored
wild waters
tumbling
round the rocks

unafraid
I made a grab for you
(couldn't resist
that smile)

don't suppose
I'll ever get
a second chance
despite standing

thigh-deep
in another river
for hours
on end casting

my line
across still waters
waiting for
a Tuesday call

and a single splash
disturbs
the surface
of that black-silk pool

Kissing

frog-kisses
squashy wet baby-kisses
raspberry-flavoured sweet-tooth-kisses
a father's kiss
a lover's kiss
I've tried them all

I'd be a liar
if I said I didn't miss
the *Good-nights,* he
in his chair with the cat
our brisk greetings
every morning

fairytale kisses
don't work, believe me
you can't wake a man
from the dead
no matter how hard
you try

these days
my heart lifts
at a row of email *xxxxx's*
and a new-old name
in the sender line
a frog-prince?

Secrets

some secrets are known
only to birds
      the way they
      whiffle
pulling air from their wings
thumb a lift on thermals
piecing together the jigsaw
of each new day
      learn
the architecture
of ancient nest-patterns
or tumble into last year's builds
with unerring accuracy
      map
the geometry of a shoreline
navigate by magnetic fields
to drift on the salt-air
of moon-drawn tides
      rehearse
the tunes of their fathers
performing on the wing
to dazzle with song-lines
from memory's inner ear

we too hold our secrets
      the way we
      recognise
            a voice on the phone
after 25 years of silence

Evil eye

crows are chasing
one-on-one
across the morning sky
for a moment
they pause
step with delicate feet
onto a thin branch
inching along
one to the other
malevolence
in each yellow stare
open beaks mouthing
black-winged curses
(too late for garlic)
as in the far distance
a baby lies in his cot
struggling for breath
no quarter from the birds
they've marked his card
bewitching
his final minutes
ready to escort him
where meteors roll
and doors are sealed
entry strictly forbidden
until the appointed hour
all in a day's work
for the crows
who fly home
freewheeling
across white-winter fields

Black magic

I was too young
and too small
to understand
the whispered curse
Blood and bones
and snow be upon
your baby head,
a head so small
my mother had
a silk bonnet
made specially
for my christening

no mention
of the curse
or who and what
whirled round my cot
with evil intention
bats, black crows
blue arctic snows …
the years go by
my red blood
keeps pumping,
white bones
stay strong

come the winter,
come the night
snow falling
flake by flake
snow-storm
snow-blizzard
snow-blindness
the sing-song
of forgotten witches

Blood and bones
and snow be upon
your old grey head

Singing the blues

Can I hold your hand?
I look up at the young man
in his dark blue top,
smile back – after all
we've just met –
but it's a long time
since I've had
such a good offer.

I settle on the pillow
pull on a blue hairnet
take in my surroundings
a wide window, white
with summer sunshine
a rack of bottles
box of blue gloves
winking instruments.

A felt-tip spot marks
my left eye, filled now
with blinding drops.
A doctor bustles in
drapes a blue mask
with a spy-hole
across my face, prepares
to inject into my eye.

I don't feel the sting,
I'm too busy enjoying
the warmth of a man's hand
holding mine.

One lady owner

Take your card, Bird, she says,
on auto-pilot, her attention
already on the truck driver
behind me, forearms tattooed
with *Love ya Babe* in red.
Thanks. I make for my car.

Filled to the brim,
I drive home, the day winter-
clear, road blurred. Radio 4
lunchtime news, a NATO
serviceman killed, *His family
has been informed.*

My eyes, my bloody eyes!
I park my car, switch off,
throw keys into the drawer,
head full of the dead soldier.
Has he got kids? I wonder,
Did they make it to school?

A last patrol, a 2am knock,
just his bad luck
he trod where he did.
A last fill-up, my eyes
drawing the short straw –
a small death
          in the circumstances.

Misunderstanding

We're in an anonymous
B&Q-type display kitchen,
my coffee percolator
the only thing I recognise –
and we're arguing,
(but we never argue)
What the hell possessed you?
I leave you on your own
for five minutes (nine years)
and you go and do
a stupid thing like this!
You perch on the edge
of the worktop, glare at me,
pushing at your spectacles
with fourth finger, left hand.
Without a by-your-leave
or word of warning –
I don't understand you these days.
You jump down, take me
by the shoulders, look me
squarely in the eye. *I'm sorry,*
I say, *I didn't want to do it –*
in fact, it was bloody hard,
I'm almost in tears, see
the blue flanks, number plate,
hear the click of a seat-belt.
Can't you buy it back?
you ask. *It's no use –*
I can't drive any more.
That stops you in your tracks.
Why on earth not? It's my eyes,
I say, *I can't see properly.*
You pull me close, cup my face,
Why didn't you tell me?
I tried, I say, *You didn't listen.*

Your old self, you feather
my cheek with thick fingers.
Like a coffee – or are you still
a tea-man? No reply,
but I feel your warmth, well
I think I do, wake to find
the cat whiskering my face.

Last orders

It comes to all of us,
last spring,
    last sight of the moon,
        last words.
These days my last things
    are coming
        thick and fast.

My father photographed
a lone gull,
    all aggressive yellow bill,
        fierce round eye,
perched on the rail
of a Clyde steamer
on his final trip to Dunoon –
not that he knew it
    at the time.

My husband drove me
to Llandaff the day
    before he died,
        determined
to buy me an Easter present –
Gary Rhodes, Step-by-Step Cookery
I keep it on a shelf
    in the kitchen.

Eyes shutting down,
colours fading to grey,
    sharp edges misting,
        my poems
are disappearing
    like spectres glimmering
        in the night.
And I'll have parked my car
    in the driveway
        for the last time.

Indigo Dreams Publishing
24, Forest Houses
Halwill
Beaworthy
Devon
EX21 5UU
www.indigodreams.co.uk